100 Interesting Facts About Mexico

A Collection of Amazing Facts About Mexico

Introduction

Welcome to "100 Amazing Facts About Mexico for Young Readers!" Get ready to explore a land bursting with vibrant colors, rich history, and incredible wonders. From ancient pyramids and lively festivals to delicious cuisine and amazing wildlife, Mexico is full of surprises. Dive into this book and discover what makes Mexico a truly enchanting place!

Chapter 1: History and Heritage

- Fact 1: Ancient Civilizations

- Fact 2: Spanish Conquest

- Fact 3: Independence from Spain

- Fact 4: Mexican Revolution

- Fact 5: Modern Mexico

Fact 1: Ancient Civilizations

Mexico boasts a legacy of ancient civilizations, including the Olmec, Maya, and Aztec cultures. These civilizations built magnificent cities, developed sophisticated writing systems, and made significant advancements in mathematics, astronomy, and art. Their pyramids and temples stand as testament to their architectural prowess, while their knowledge of astronomy allowed them to create precise calendars.

Fact 2: Spanish Conquest

In the early 16th century, Spanish conquistadors, led by Hernán Cortés, conquered the Aztec Empire, which was a pivotal event marking the beginning of Spanish colonization in Mexico. This conquest brought profound changes to the region's indigenous peoples and cultures, reshaping political structures, introducing new religious beliefs, and altering social dynamics. The impact of Spanish colonization laid the foundation for modern Mexico's cultural and historical evolution.

Fact 3: Independence from Spain

Mexico gained its independence from Spain on September 16, 1810, after a decade-long struggle led by figures like Miguel Hidalgo and José María Morelos. The declaration of independence marked a significant turning point in Mexican history, paving the way for Mexico to establish itself as a sovereign nation. This event ended over three centuries of Spanish colonial rule and ignited a process of nation-building that continues to shape Mexico's identity and cultural heritage today.

Fact 4: Mexican Revolution

The Mexican Revolution began in 1910, sparked by social inequality, land disputes, and a desire for political reform. Led by figures such as Emiliano Zapata and Pancho Villa, the revolution sought to overthrow the dictatorship of Porfirio Díaz and resulted in significant social and political changes, including the redistribution of land and the establishment of labor rights. This transformative period reshaped Mexico's societal structure and laid the groundwork for modern reforms and policies.

Fact 5: Modern Mexico

Today, Mexico is a vibrant blend of ancient traditions and modern influences. It is known for its diverse culture, from colorful festivals like Día de los Muertos (Day of the Dead) to its contributions to global arts, cuisine, and technology sectors. Mexico continues to evolve while celebrating its rich heritage, embracing innovation in industries such as automotive manufacturing and telecommunications, while also preserving its indigenous languages and cultural practices.

Chapter 2: Natural Wonders

- Fact 6: Sumidero Canyon

- Fact 7: Hierve el Agua

- Fact 8: Cenotes of Yucatan

- Fact 9: Pico de Orizaba

- Fact 10: El Pinacate and Gran Desierto de Altar

Fact 6: Sumidero Canyon

Sumidero Canyon (Cañón del Sumidero) is a stunning natural wonder located in the state of Chiapas, Mexico. Carved by the Grijalva River, the canyon features towering cliffs rising up to 1,000 meters (3,280 feet) above the riverbed. It is renowned for its dramatic landscapes, diverse wildlife, and opportunities for boat tours to explore its majestic depths.

Fact 7: Hierve el Agua

Hierve el Agua, located in the state of Oaxaca, is a unique natural formation featuring mineral-laden springs that cascade over cliffs, creating petrified waterfalls. These "waterfalls" resemble frozen water but are actually mineral deposits formed over thousands of years. Hierve el Agua also offers stunning panoramic views of the surrounding valleys and mountains.

Fact 8: Cenotes of Yucatan

The cenotes of Yucatán Peninsula are natural sinkholes or underground rivers formed by the collapse of limestone bedrock. These cenotes are filled with crystal-clear freshwater and are significant in Mayan culture as sacred sites and sources of water. They offer unique opportunities for swimming, diving, and exploring the intricate underground cave systems.

Fact 9: Pico de Orizaba

Pico de Orizaba, also known as Citlaltépetl, is Mexico's highest peak and the third highest in North America. Located on the border between the states of Puebla and Veracruz, this dormant volcano rises to an elevation of 5,636 meters (18,491 feet) above sea level. It is a popular destination for mountaineers and offers breathtaking views of the surrounding landscape.

Fact 10: El Pinacate and Gran Desierto de Altar

El Pinacate and Gran Desierto de Altar Biosphere Reserve, located in the state of Sonora, is known for its volcanic landscapes and vast sand dunes. It encompasses a diverse range of ecosystems, including volcanic craters, lava fields, desert flora, and unique wildlife adapted to extreme desert conditions.

Chapter 3: Geography

- Fact 11: Diverse Landscapes

- Fact 12: Natural Wonders

- Fact 13: Climate Variations

- Fact 14: Biodiversity

- Fact 15: Geological Features

Fact 11: Diverse Landscapes

Mexico boasts incredibly diverse landscapes, ranging from lush tropical rainforests in regions like Chiapas and the Yucatán Peninsula to arid deserts in the north, such as the Chihuahuan Desert. The country also features towering mountain ranges like the Sierra Madre Occidental and the Sierra Madre Oriental, offering breathtaking scenery and diverse ecosystems.

Fact 12: Natural Wonders

Mexico is home to numerous natural wonders, including the stunning Copper Canyon (Barranca del Cobre), which is larger and deeper than the Grand Canyon in the United States. Other notable natural marvels include the Monarch Butterfly Biosphere Reserve, where millions of monarch butterflies migrate annually, and the underground rivers and cenotes (natural sinkholes) of the Yucatán Peninsula.

Fact 13: Climate Variations

Due to its diverse geography, Mexico experiences a wide range of climates, from tropical and subtropical climates in the south to temperate and even alpine climates in the central highlands. Coastal areas are influenced by the Pacific Ocean and the Gulf of Mexico, contributing to variations in temperature and precipitation throughout the country.

Fact 14: Biodiversity

Mexico is one of the world's most biodiverse countries, hosting a vast array of plant and animal species. The country is home to over 200,000 species, including iconic animals like jaguars, monarch butterflies, and quetzal birds. Its rich biodiversity is preserved in numerous protected areas, such as biosphere reserves and national parks, ensuring the conservation of its natural heritage for future generations to enjoy and study.

Fact 15: Geological Features

Mexico's geological features are as varied as its landscapes, with notable formations like the volcanic peaks of Popocatépetl and Iztaccíhuatl near Mexico City. The country also features unique geological formations such as the limestone caves and cenotes of the Yucatán Peninsula, formed by the dissolution of soluble rocks over millions of years. These geological marvels not only contribute to Mexico's natural beauty but also provide insights into its geological history and environmental diversity.

Chapter 4: People and Society

- Fact 16: Population Diversity

- Fact 17: Family and Community Life

- Fact 18: Education System

- Fact 19: Social Issues and Challenges

- Fact 20: Famous Mexicans

Fact 16: Population Diversity

Mexico is a melting pot of cultures, with a population that reflects its indigenous roots, Spanish heritage, and diverse immigrant communities. The country's population includes indigenous groups such as the Maya and Zapotec, mestizos (people of mixed European and indigenous ancestry), and people of European, African, and Asian descent. This cultural diversity enriches Mexico's societal fabric, contributing to its vibrant arts, cuisine, languages, and traditions celebrated both nationally and globally.

Fact 17: Family and Community Life

Family plays a central role in Mexican society, with strong bonds among extended families and close-knit communities. Traditional values emphasize respect for elders, hospitality, and solidarity during celebrations and times of hardship. Festivals like Día de los Muertos (Day of the Dead) and religious holidays often strengthen family ties and community spirit.

Fact 18: Education System

Mexico's education system is structured into three levels: primary, secondary, and higher education. While education is mandatory up to the secondary level, access and quality vary across regions. Efforts are ongoing to improve educational opportunities, including initiatives to modernize curriculum, enhance teacher training, and expand access to digital resources.

Fact 19: Social Issues and Challenges

Mexico faces social challenges such as poverty, inequality, and crime, particularly in urban areas and marginalized communities. Issues like access to healthcare, environmental sustainability, and human rights remain priorities for social development. Civil society organizations and government initiatives work to address these challenges and promote social justice.

Fact 20: Famous Mexicans

Mexico has produced many influential figures in various fields, including arts, sciences, and sports. Notable individuals include renowned artists, Nobel Prize-winning scientists, and legendary athletes. These figures have made significant contributions to their respective fields and have had a lasting impact on both Mexican and global culture.

Chapter 5: Places to Visit

- Fact 21: Mexico City and its Attractions

- Fact 22: Ancient Ruins of Teotihuacan

- Fact 23: Beaches of Cancun and the Riviera Maya

- Fact 24: Chichen Itza and Mayan Culture

- Fact 25: Colonial Cities like Guanajuato and Oaxaca

Fact 21: Mexico City and its Attractions

Mexico City, the capital, is one of the largest cities in the world and boasts a rich cultural heritage. Attractions include the historic center (Zócalo), which is one of the largest public squares globally and surrounded by historic buildings such as the National Palace and Templo Mayor. Chapultepec Park, one of the largest urban parks in the Western Hemisphere, features museums like the National Museum of Anthropology and the Chapultepec Castle, offering panoramic views of the city.

Fact 22: Ancient Ruins of Teotihuacan

Teotihuacan, located near Mexico City, is home to impressive ancient ruins, including the Pyramid of the Sun and the Pyramid of the Moon. It was once a thriving city of the Mesoamerican civilization and is now an archaeological marvel. This site attracts visitors from around the world who come to explore its monumental pyramids, intricate murals, and learn about the ancient culture that flourished there.

Fact 23: Beaches of Cancun and the Riviera Maya

Cancun and the Riviera Maya are famous for their stunning beaches along the Caribbean coast. Visitors can enjoy white sand beaches, crystal-clear waters, and opportunities for snorkeling, diving, and exploring nearby Mayan ruins like Tulum. These destinations offer a perfect blend of relaxation and exploration, where travelers can immerse themselves in natural beauty while discovering the rich cultural heritage of the Mayan civilization.

Fact 24: Chichen Itza and Mayan Culture

Chichen Itza is a prominent archaeological site in the Yucatán Peninsula, known for its well-preserved Mayan ruins such as the El Castillo pyramid. This ancient city served as an economic and cultural hub for the Maya, featuring impressive structures that highlight their astronomical knowledge, architectural prowess, and cultural practices.

Fact 25: Colonial Cities like Guanajuato and Oaxaca

Mexico boasts beautiful colonial cities like Guanajuato and Oaxaca, known for their colorful architecture, cobblestone streets, and cultural festivals. Guanajuato is famous for its underground streets and vibrant arts scene, while Oaxaca is renowned for its indigenous crafts and cuisine. These cities offer visitors a glimpse into Mexico's rich colonial history and vibrant cultural heritage, making them popular destinations for travelers seeking both history and cultural immersion.

Chapter 6: Travel Tips

- Fact 26: Currency and Money Tips

- Fact 27: Transportation Options

- Fact 28: Safety Advice for Travelers

- Fact 29: Language Tips

- Fact 30: Cultural Etiquette

Fact 26: Currency and Money Tips

Mexico's currency is the Mexican Peso (MXN). It's recommended to exchange currency at banks or exchange offices for better rates than at airports or hotels. Credit cards are widely accepted in tourist areas, but it's good to have some cash for smaller establishments. ATMs are also widely available for convenient currency withdrawal, but be mindful of transaction fees and safety precautions when using them.

Fact 27: Transportation Options

In Mexico, transportation options include taxis, buses (including long-distance luxury buses), metro systems in major cities like Mexico City, and rideshare services like Uber. Consider local conditions and safety when choosing transportation. It's advisable to use official taxi services or trusted rideshare apps for safety and convenience, especially in urban areas.

Fact 28: Safety Advice for Travelers

Exercise caution in Mexico regarding personal safety. Stick to well-traveled areas, avoid displaying valuables, use reputable transportation services, and stay informed about local news and safety alerts. Always keep important documents secure, such as passports and identification, and consider registering with your embassy or consulate for additional safety information and assistance while traveling.

Fact 29: Language Tips

While Spanish is the official language of Mexico, English is widely spoken in tourist areas. Learning a few basic Spanish phrases can enhance your experience and interactions with locals. Locals appreciate efforts to speak their language, even if it's just a few words, and it can also help you navigate situations where English may not be as commonly understood.

Fact 30: Cultural Etiquette

In Mexican culture, it's customary to greet with a handshake or a light hug (for closer acquaintances). Respect personal space and avoid sensitive topics like politics or religion unless invited to discuss. Always ask before taking photos of people, especially in indigenous communities, as it shows respect for their culture and privacy. Remember to address people politely using "señor" (Mr.) or "señora" (Mrs.) followed by their last name unless invited to use their first name.

Chapter 7: Famous Cities

- Fact 31: Monterrey, the Industrial Hub

- Fact 32: Puebla and its Culinary Delights

- Fact 33: Guadalajara, the City of Mariachi

- Fact 34: Tijuana, Border City Vibes

- Fact 35: Mérida, Yucatán's Cultural Capital

Fact 31: Monterrey, the Industrial Hub

Monterrey, located in northeastern Mexico, is known as the country's industrial and business center. It boasts a strong economy with numerous multinational corporations and manufacturing plants. The city is also surrounded by scenic mountains, offering outdoor activities such as hiking and rock climbing. Monterrey is famous for its modern infrastructure, vibrant cultural scene, and educational institutions, making it a dynamic and progressive city.

Fact 32: Puebla and its Culinary Delights

Puebla, situated southeast of Mexico City, is famous for its rich culinary heritage. The city is the birthplace of dishes like mole poblano and chiles en nogada. Puebla's historic center features beautiful colonial architecture and vibrant talavera pottery. The city also hosts the annual Cinco de Mayo celebrations, commemorating the Battle of Puebla, where Mexican forces defeated the French army in 1862.

Fact 33: Guadalajara, the City of Mariachi

Guadalajara, the capital of the state of Jalisco, is known for its mariachi music and tequila. The city hosts the annual International Mariachi Festival and is a cultural hub with numerous theaters, museums, and galleries. Guadalajara is also home to the famous Hospicio Cabañas. The city's rich history and lively arts scene make it a vibrant and exciting destination for visitors.

Fact 34: Tijuana, Border City Vibes

Tijuana, located on the US-Mexico border, offers a unique blend of Mexican and American cultures. Known for its lively nightlife, diverse cuisine, and vibrant arts scene, Tijuana is a popular destination for tourists. The city's bustling markets and street art reflect its dynamic and ever-evolving identity. Tijuana also serves as a gateway for travelers exploring the Baja California region, making it a vital cultural and commercial hub.

Fact 35: Mérida, Yucatán's Cultural Capital

Mérida, the capital of the Yucatán Peninsula, is celebrated for its rich Mayan and colonial heritage. The city is known for its historic mansions, bustling markets, and cultural festivals. Mérida's vibrant arts scene includes traditional Yucatecan music and dance, as well as contemporary art and theater. The city's proximity to Mayan archaeological sites and natural wonders, such as cenotes and biosphere reserves, makes it a fascinating destination for history enthusiasts and nature lovers alike.

Chapter 8: Culture and Traditions

- Fact 36: Day of the Dead

- Fact 37: Mariachi Music

- Fact 38: Traditional Dances

- Fact 39: Mexican Cuisine

- Fact 40: Mexican Festivals

Fact 36: Day of the Dead

The Day of the Dead, or Día de los Muertos, is a vibrant and colorful Mexican holiday celebrated on November 1st and 2nd. It is a time to honor and remember deceased loved ones through various traditions, including building altars (ofrendas) adorned with photos, candles, marigold flowers, and favorite foods of the departed. Families visit cemeteries to clean and decorate graves, and they celebrate with music, dance, and traditional foods. This holiday showcases Mexico's rich cultural heritage.

Fact 37: Mariachi Music

Mariachi music is a quintessential part of Mexican culture. Originating in the western states of Mexico, particularly Jalisco, this genre features ensembles that typically include violins, trumpets, guitars, vihuelas, and guitarróns. Mariachi bands perform at various celebrations and events, playing lively and emotional songs that capture the essence of Mexican life and traditions. The musicians often wear charro suits, adding to the visual appeal of their performances.

Fact 38: Traditional Dances

Traditional Mexican dances are an integral part of the country's cultural expression, with each region having its own unique styles and forms. One of the most famous dances is the Jarabe Tapatío, also known as the Mexican Hat Dance, which is a symbol of national pride. Other popular dances include the Danza de los Viejitos from Michoacán, the Sones from Veracruz, and the Concheros dance, which has indigenous roots.

Fact 39: Modern BuildingsMexican Cuisine

Mexican cuisine is renowned worldwide for its rich flavors, diverse ingredients, and vibrant dishes. It is a blend of indigenous Mesoamerican cooking with Spanish influences. Staples of Mexican cuisine include corn, beans, chili peppers, and a variety of spices. Popular dishes include tacos, enchiladas, tamales, mole, and pozole. Mexican cuisine also features an array of salsas and sauces, each adding unique flavors to meals.

Fact 40: Mexican Festivals

Mexico is known for its lively and colorful festivals, each reflecting the country's rich cultural traditions and history. One of the most famous is Cinco de Mayo, which commemorates the Battle of Puebla and Mexican resistance against French forces. Another significant festival is Guelaguetza in Oaxaca, celebrating indigenous cultures with traditional dances, music, and costumes. These festivals, along with many others, are vital expressions of Mexican identity and community spirit.

Chapter 9: Famous Landmarks

- Fact 41: El Castillo at Chichen Itza

- Fact 42: The Angel of Independence

- Fact 43: Frida Kahlo Museum

- Fact 44: The Zocalo

- Fact 45: Chapultepec Castle

Fact 41: El Castillo at Chichen Itza

El Castillo, also known as the Temple of Kukulcán, is a magnificent step-pyramid located at the ancient Mayan city of Chichen Itza in the Yucatán Peninsula. It was built by the Maya civilization between the 9th and 12th centuries and served as a temple to the god Kukulcán. The pyramid is renowned for its precise architecture and astronomical significance, particularly during the equinoxes when shadows create the illusion of a serpent descending down the stairs.

Fact 42: The Angel of Independence

The Angel of Independence (El Ángel de la Independencia) is a iconic victory column located on Paseo de la Reforma in Mexico City. Built in 1910 to commemorate the centennial of the beginning of Mexico's War of Independence, it stands as a symbol of freedom and victory. The column is topped with a golden angel holding a laurel wreath and a broken chain, representing Mexico's independence from Spanish colonial rule.

Fact 43: Frida Kahlo Museum

The Frida Kahlo Museum (Museo Frida Kahlo), also known as the Blue House (Casa Azul), is located in Coyoacán, Mexico City. It was the birthplace and lifelong home of the renowned Mexican artist Frida Kahlo. Today, the museum houses a collection of Kahlo's artwork, personal belongings, and artifacts that offer insight into her life, art, and political activism. It is a significant cultural landmark preserving Kahlo's legacy and contributions to art and Mexican culture.

Fact 44: The Zocalo

The Zócalo, officially known as Plaza de la Constitución, is the main square in the heart of Mexico City's historic center. It has been a central gathering place since Aztec times when it was the ceremonial center of the city of Tenochtitlan. Today, the Zócalo is surrounded by historic buildings such as the Metropolitan Cathedral, National Palace, and Templo Mayor archaeological site. It hosts cultural events, celebrations, and protests, making it a vibrant symbol of Mexico's past and present.

Fact 45: Chapultepec Castle

Chapultepec Castle (Castillo de Chapultepec) is located on Chapultepec Hill in Mexico City's Chapultepec Park. Originally built as a retreat for Aztec rulers, it later became the residence of Mexican presidents and emperors. The castle is notable for its panoramic views of Mexico City and its historic significance as the site of battles during the Mexican-American War. Today, it houses the National Museum of History, showcasing artifacts and exhibits related to Mexico's history and culture.

Chapter 10: Language

- Fact 46: Spanish as the National Language

- Fact 47: Indigenous Languages

- Fact 48: Family LifeNahuatl Words in English

- Fact 49: Regional Dialects

- Fact 50: Language Preservation Efforts

Fact 46: Spanish as the National Language

Spanish is the official and national language of Mexico. Introduced by Spanish colonizers during the 16th century, it has since become the predominant language spoken by the majority of the population. Spanish in Mexico exhibits unique characteristics and regional variations, reflecting its evolution within the country's diverse cultural and geographical landscapes.

Fact 47: Indigenous Languages

Mexico is also home to a rich diversity of indigenous languages, with over 68 recognized languages spoken by indigenous communities across the country. These languages are an important part of Mexico's cultural heritage and identity, reflecting the linguistic diversity that existed long before Spanish colonization. Efforts to preserve and promote these indigenous languages are ongoing, recognizing their significance in maintaining Mexico's cultural mosaic and ancestral traditions.

Fact 48: Nahuatl Words in English

Nahuatl, the language of the Aztec Empire, has contributed several words to the English language. Examples include "avocado," "chili," "chocolate," "tomato," and "coyote." These words were adopted into English through Spanish, which borrowed them from Nahuatl during the colonial period. The influence of Nahuatl extends beyond vocabulary, enriching global culinary and cultural lexicons.

Fact 49: Regional Dialects

Within Mexico, there are numerous regional dialects and variations of Spanish spoken. These dialects can vary significantly in pronunciation, vocabulary, and grammar from one region to another. Some well-known regional dialects include those spoken in Yucatán, Oaxaca, and northern Mexico, each contributing to the rich linguistic tapestry of the country.

Fact 50: Language Preservation Efforts

Efforts to preserve and promote indigenous languages in Mexico have gained momentum in recent years. Various initiatives aim to document and revitalize endangered languages, support language education programs in indigenous communities, and foster pride in linguistic diversity. Organizations and government policies play crucial roles in these preservation efforts to ensure the continuity of Mexico's indigenous languages.

Chapter 11: Economy

- Fact 51: Major Industries

- Fact 52: Agriculture

- Fact 53: Trade Agreements

- Fact 54: Tourism Industry

- Fact 55: Mexican Peso

Fact 51: Major Industries

Mexico's major industries include automotive manufacturing, electronics, petroleum, textiles, and food and beverages. Automotive manufacturing, in particular, is a significant sector, with Mexico being one of the world's largest producers of vehicles and auto parts. This industry has attracted substantial foreign investment and plays a crucial role in Mexico's export economy.

Fact 52: Agriculture

Agriculture plays a vital role in Mexico's economy, with a diverse range of crops grown across the country. Major agricultural products include corn, beans, sugarcane, coffee, tomatoes, avocados, and citrus fruits. Mexico is also a leading producer of tropical fruits and vegetables, contributing significantly to both domestic consumption and international markets.

Fact 53: Trade Agreements

Mexico is a prominent participant in international trade agreements. It is a member of the United States-Mexico-Canada Agreement (USMCA), which replaced the North American Free Trade Agreement (NAFTA). Mexico also has trade agreements with numerous countries and regions worldwide, facilitating global commerce and economic integration.

Fact 54: Tourism Industry

Mexico's tourism industry is a significant economic driver, attracting millions of visitors each year to its diverse attractions. Popular destinations include beach resorts in Cancún, historical sites like Chichen Itza and Teotihuacan, cultural hubs such as Mexico City and Oaxaca, and natural wonders like the Copper Canyon and Riviera Maya.

Fact 55: Mexican Peso

The Mexican Peso (MXN) is the official currency of Mexico, symbolized by the "$" sign, and subdivided into 100 centavos. The peso's exchange rate fluctuates based on economic conditions and international market factors, impacting both domestic and international trade. This fluctuation influences Mexico's import and export competitiveness and affects the purchasing power of its citizens and businesses in the global economy.

Chapter 12: Sports

- Fact 56: Soccer - The National Sport

- Fact 57: Baseball Popularity

- Fact 58: Lucha Libre Wrestling

- Fact 59: Bullfighting Tradition

- Fact 60: Famous Mexican Athletes

Fact 56: Soccer - The National Sport

Soccer, known as football (fútbol) in Mexico, is the national sport and enjoys widespread popularity across the country. Mexico has a strong soccer tradition, with the national team (El Tri) being a source of national pride and competing in international tournaments like the FIFA World Cup, uniting fans nationwide with fervent support.

Fact 57: Baseball Popularity

Baseball holds significant popularity in Mexico, particularly in regions like the northern states. The Mexican Baseball League (LMB) is a professional league with a devoted fan base, and Mexico has produced notable players who have achieved success in Major League Baseball (MLB) in the United States, showcasing Mexico's deep-rooted passion for the sport on an international stage.

Fact 58: Lucha Libre Wrestling

Lucha Libre, or Mexican wrestling, is a colorful and theatrical form of professional wrestling. Known for its masked wrestlers (luchadores) and acrobatic moves, Lucha Libre has a dedicated following in Mexico and has influenced wrestling styles worldwide, blending athleticism with entertainment. Its vibrant characters and high-flying maneuvers have made it a cultural phenomenon that transcends borders, captivating audiences both in Mexico and internationally.

Fact 59: Bullfighting Tradition

Bullfighting has a long-standing tradition in Mexico, dating back to the Spanish colonial era. It remains a significant cultural event in some regions, particularly in cities like Mexico City, where bullfights are held during certain festivals. However, it has also been a topic of debate regarding animal rights and ethical concerns, prompting discussions about its future and cultural significance in modern Mexican society.

Fact 60: Famous Mexican Athletes

Mexico has produced many renowned athletes across various sports. Some famous Mexican athletes include Hugo Sánchez (soccer), Fernando Valenzuela (baseball), Lorena Ochoa (golf), Ana Guevara (athletics), and Saúl "Canelo" Álvarez (boxing), among others, who have achieved international acclaim and contributed to Mexico's sporting legacy.

Chapter 13: Environment

- Fact 61: National Parks

- Fact 62: Conservation Efforts

- Fact 63: Biodiversity

- Fact 64: Environmental Challenges

- Fact 65: Renewable Energy

Fact 61: National Parks

Mexico boasts 182 national parks, which protect its diverse landscapes and ecosystems. These parks range from tropical rainforests in the Yucatán Peninsula to arid deserts in Baja California. Notable examples include the Monarch Butterfly Biosphere Reserve and the Sierra de las Minas Biosphere Reserve, known for its rich biodiversity.

Fact 62: Conservation Efforts

Mexico is actively involved in various conservation programs aimed at preserving its natural resources. The country has established numerous protected areas and wildlife reserves. Organizations like the Mexican National Commission for Protected Natural Areas (CONANP) work to protect endangered species, restore habitats, and promote sustainable practices among local communities.

Fact 63: Biodiversity

Mexico is one of the world's most biodiverse countries, ranking fifth globally in terms of plant and animal species. It is home to more than 200,000 species, including unique animals like the axolotl and the Mexican gray wolf. The country's diverse ecosystems, from coral reefs to cloud forests, support this incredible variety of life.

Fact 64: Environmental Challenges

Despite its efforts, Mexico faces several environmental challenges, including deforestation, air pollution, and water scarcity. Rapid urbanization and industrialization have led to habitat loss and increased greenhouse gas emissions. The government and various organizations are working to address these issues through policies and community initiatives aimed at reducing environmental impact.

Fact 65: Renewable Energy

Mexico is investing heavily in renewable energy sources to reduce its reliance on fossil fuels. The country has significant potential for solar and wind energy, particularly in the northern and southern regions. Recent initiatives include large-scale solar farms and wind turbines, which are part of Mexico's commitment to sustainable energy and reducing greenhouse gas emissions.

Chapter 14: Holidays and Celebrations

- act 66: Day of the Dead

- Fact 67: Cinco de Mayo

- Fact 68: Mexican Independence Day

- Fact 69: Las Posadas

- Fact 70: Guelaguetza

Fact 66: Day of the Dead

The Day of the Dead is a vibrant Mexican holiday celebrated on November 1st and 2nd. This tradition honors deceased loved ones with colorful altars, marigold flowers, and offerings of food and personal mementos. It blends indigenous practices with Catholicism and is deeply rooted in Mexican culture.

Fact 67. Cinco de Mayo

Cinco de Mayo, celebrated on May 5th, commemorates the Mexican Army's victory over the French forces at the Battle of Puebla in 1862. Contrary to popular belief, it is not Mexico's Independence Day but a regional holiday with festivities that include parades, music, and traditional Mexican foods, especially in Puebla and among Mexican communities in the United States.

Fact 68: Mexican Independence Day

Mexican Independence Day, observed on September 16th, marks the start of Mexico's fight for independence from Spain in 1810. The celebration begins on the night of September 15th with "El Grito de Dolores," a reenactment of the call to arms by Miguel Hidalgo. Festivities include parades, fireworks, and patriotic displays of the Mexican flag.

Fact 69: Las Posadas

Las Posadas is a traditional Christmas celebration held from December 16th to 24th. The event reenacts Mary and Joseph's search for lodging in Bethlehem. Participants, often dressed in biblical costumes, go from house to house singing carols and asking for shelter. The celebration ends with a party featuring piñatas, food, and drinks.

Fact 70: Guelaguetza

The Guelaguetza is a cultural festival held in Oaxaca every July. It showcases the region's indigenous cultures through traditional music, dance, and costumes. The festival is renowned for its vibrant parades, folk dances, and culinary delights, celebrating the rich cultural heritage of Oaxaca and its diverse ethnic groups.

Chapter 15: Science and Innovation

- Fact 71: Mexico's Space Program

- Fact 72: Innovations in Agriculture

- Fact 73: Medical Advancements

- Fact 74: Contributions to Astronomy

- Fact 75: Green Technology

Fact 71: Mexico's Space Program

Mexico's space program, managed by the Mexican Space Agency (AEM), has made significant strides since its establishment in 2010. The country has launched satellites for Earth observation, telecommunications, and scientific research. Notable achievements include the launch of the Centenario satellite and the development of Mexico's own satellite technologies, contributing to advancements in space science and communications.

Fact 72: Innovations in Agriculture

Mexico has pioneered various agricultural innovations to boost productivity and sustainability. Techniques such as precision farming and the development of drought-resistant crops are transforming agriculture in the country. Programs focusing on organic farming and sustainable practices are also gaining traction, helping to increase yields while preserving the environment.

Fact 73: Medical Advancements

Mexico has made notable advancements in medical research and healthcare. The country is known for its contributions to the development of vaccines and treatments for diseases such as diabetes and cancer. Institutions like the National Institute of Genomic Medicine (INMEGEN) and the National Institute of Public Health (INSP) play a crucial role in advancing medical research and improving public health.

Fact 74: Contributions to Astronomy

Mexico has made significant contributions to astronomy, including the establishment of the National Astronomical Observatory. Mexican scientists and institutions have been involved in major astronomical projects, such as the study of cosmic rays and the development of advanced telescopes. The country is also home to the Large Millimeter Telescope (LMT), one of the world's largest and most powerful radio telescopes.

Fact 75: Green Technology

Mexico is investing heavily in green technology to address environmental challenges and promote sustainability. The country is developing and implementing renewable energy sources, such as solar and wind power, to reduce dependence on fossil fuels. Initiatives include the expansion of solar energy farms and the promotion of energy-efficient technologies in various sectors.

Chapter 16: Traditional Clothing

- Fact 76: The Charro Suit

- Fact 77: The Huipil

- Fact 78: The Rebozo

- Fact 79: Traditional Embroidery

- Fact 80: Day of the Dead Costumes

Fact 76: The Charro Suit

The Charro suit is a traditional Mexican outfit worn by male charros, or horsemen, during events such as rodeos and festivals. The suit features intricate embroidery, a wide-brimmed hat, and decorative silver buttons. It reflects Mexican ranching culture and is often associated with performances of traditional mariachi music.

Fact 77: The Huipil

The huipil is a traditional Mexican garment worn by women, especially in indigenous communities. It is a loose-fitting tunic, usually made from cotton or wool, and is often adorned with elaborate embroidery and patterns that represent the wearer's cultural heritage. The huipil varies in design and style depending on the region and ethnic group.

Fact 78: The Rebozo

The rebozo is a versatile Mexican shawl or wrap worn by women. It is used for various purposes, including as a cover-up, a baby carrier, or a fashion accessory. Traditionally handwoven, the rebozo comes in a range of fabrics and designs, and it holds cultural significance in Mexican dress and daily life.

Fact 79: Traditional Embroidery

Traditional embroidery in Mexico is known for its vivid colors and intricate designs. Each region has its own distinctive embroidery style, often reflecting local flora, fauna, and cultural symbols. This embroidery is commonly used on clothing such as huipils and rebozos, and is a key element of Mexican folk art.

Fact 80: Day of the Dead Costumes

During the Day of the Dead celebrations, participants often wear costumes that incorporate vibrant colors and symbolic elements. These costumes may include calavera (skull) makeup, floral headbands, and decorated clothing, reflecting the festive and respectful nature of the holiday. The attire helps to honor deceased loved ones and celebrate their lives.

Chapter 17: Food and Drink

- Fact 81: Tacos

- Fact 82: Tamales

- Fact 83: Mole

- Fact 84: Churros

- Fact 85: Mexican Hot Chocolate

Fact 81: Tacos

Tacos are a quintessential Mexican dish consisting of a tortilla filled with various ingredients such as meats, vegetables, and sauces. They can be made with soft or crispy tortillas and are often topped with fresh ingredients like cilantro, onions, and salsa. Tacos come in numerous varieties, including carne asada (grilled beef), al pastor (marinated pork), and fish tacos.

Fact 82: Tamales

Tamales are traditional Mexican foods made from masa (corn dough) filled with meats, cheeses, or vegetables, and wrapped in corn husks or banana leaves. They are typically steamed and served with salsa or sour cream. Tamales are often prepared for special occasions and holidays, reflecting the rich culinary heritage of Mexico.

Fact 83: Mole

Mole is a rich and complex sauce made from a blend of ingredients including chili peppers, spices, chocolate, and nuts. It comes in various regional variations, with Mole Poblano being one of the most famous. Mole is often served with chicken or turkey and is known for its deep, layered flavors.

Fact 84: Churros

Churros are a popular Mexican dessert consisting of fried dough sticks coated in cinnamon sugar. They are typically enjoyed with a cup of hot chocolate or coffee. Churros can also be filled with sweet fillings such as chocolate or caramel and are a favorite treat at fairs and festivals.

Fact 85: Mexican Hot Chocolate

Mexican hot chocolate is a traditional drink made from cocoa, sugar, and spices such as cinnamon and vanilla. It is often prepared using a traditional molinillo (a wooden whisk) to create a frothy texture. This rich and aromatic beverage is enjoyed warm and is commonly served with pastries or during festive occasions.

Chapter 18: Wildlife

- Fact 86: The Jaguar

- Fact 87: The Monarch Butterfly Migration

- Fact 88: The Mexican Wolf

- Fact 89: Marine Life in the Pacific Ocean

- Fact 90: Tropical Birds

Fact 86: The Jaguar

The jaguar is the largest wild cat in the Americas and is found in the tropical rainforests of southern Mexico. These majestic predators are known for their powerful build and distinctive rosette-patterned fur. Jaguars play a crucial role in maintaining the balance of their ecosystem by controlling the population of other animals.

Fact 87: The Monarch Butterfly Migration

Every year, millions of monarch butterflies undertake an incredible migration from Canada and the United States to the forests of central Mexico. This journey spans over 3,000 miles and is one of the most remarkable natural phenomena. The Monarch Butterfly Biosphere Reserve in Mexico protects these butterflies during their wintering period.

Fact 88: The Mexican Wolf

The Mexican wolf, a subspecies of the gray wolf, is native to Mexico and the southwestern United States. Once nearly extinct, conservation efforts have helped to reintroduce these wolves into their natural habitat. The Mexican wolf is known for its smaller size and distinctively colored fur, which ranges from gray to brown.

Fact 89:Marine Life in the Pacific Ocean

Mexico's Pacific coastline is teeming with diverse marine life. This region is home to a wide variety of species, including whales, dolphins, sea turtles, and numerous fish species. The Sea of Cortez, also known as the Gulf of California, is particularly renowned for its rich biodiversity and is often referred to as the "Aquarium of the World."

Fact 90: Tropical Birds

Mexico's diverse ecosystems support a vast array of tropical bird species. The country is home to over 1,000 bird species, including colorful parrots, toucans, and flamingos. Birdwatching is a popular activity in Mexico, with many regions offering opportunities to see these vibrant and exotic birds in their natural habitats.

Chapter 19: Education and Schools

- Fact 91: Primary and Secondary Education

- Fact 92: Higher Education Institutions

- Fact 93: Famous Universities

- Fact 94: Educational Achievements

- Fact 95: School Traditions

Fact 91: Education and Schools

In Mexico, education is compulsory for children from ages 6 to 15, covering both primary and secondary education. The primary education system consists of six grades, followed by three years of lower secondary education. The Mexican government has implemented various programs to improve access to quality education for all children, including those in rural and underserved areas.

Fact 92: Higher Education Institutions

Mexico has a diverse range of higher education institutions, including universities, technological institutes, and teacher training colleges. These institutions offer undergraduate and postgraduate programs in various fields such as engineering, medicine, social sciences, and the humanities. The National Autonomous University of Mexico (UNAM) is one of the largest and most prestigious universities in the country.

Fact 93:Famous Universities

Mexico is home to several renowned universities known for their academic excellence and research contributions. Some of the most famous include the National Autonomous University of Mexico (UNAM), the Monterrey Institute of Technology and Higher Education (ITESM), and the National Polytechnic Institute (IPN). These universities attract students from all over the world and play a significant role in advancing education and innovation.

Fact 94: Educational Achievements

Mexican students have achieved notable successes in various academic competitions and research fields. The country has produced scholars and researchers who have made significant contributions to science, technology, and the arts. Programs promoting STEM education (science, technology, engineering, and mathematics) have been particularly successful in encouraging young talent and fostering innovation.

Fact 95: School Traditions

Mexican schools have a rich tradition of cultural and social activities that complement academic learning. Events such as Independence Day celebrations, cultural festivals, and sports competitions are an integral part of school life. These traditions help to build a sense of community and pride among students, while also promoting cultural awareness and teamwork.

Chapter 20: Future Prospects

- Fact 96: Technological Advancements

- Fact 97: Sustainable Development

- Fact 98: Educational Reforms

- Fact 99: Economic Growth

- Fact 100: Taiwan's Role in the Global Community

Fact 96: Technological Advancements

Mexico is poised to become a leader in technological innovation in the coming years. The country is investing in the development of cutting-edge technologies such as artificial intelligence, biotechnology, and robotics. With a growing number of tech startups and increased support for research and development, Mexico is set to make significant strides in the global tech industry.

Fact 97: Sustainable Development

Sustainable development is a key focus for Mexico's future. The country is implementing policies and initiatives aimed at reducing carbon emissions, promoting renewable energy, and conserving natural resources. Projects such as expanding solar and wind energy farms and enhancing sustainable agricultural practices are integral to Mexico's commitment to environmental sustainability.

Fact 98: Educational Reforms

Educational reforms are crucial for Mexico's future growth and development. The government is working to improve the quality of education at all levels, with a focus on increasing access to higher education and vocational training. These reforms aim to equip students with the skills and knowledge needed to succeed in a rapidly changing global economy.

Fact 99: Economic Growth

Mexico's economy is expected to continue its growth trajectory, driven by diverse sectors such as manufacturing, tourism, and services. Trade agreements, infrastructure development, and foreign investment are key factors contributing to economic expansion. By fostering innovation and entrepreneurship, Mexico aims to strengthen its economic position on the global stage.

Fact 100: Taiwan's Role in the Global Community

Mexico is playing an increasingly significant role in the global community. As a member of international organizations like the United Nations and the World Trade Organization, Mexico is actively involved in global decision-making processes. The country is also strengthening its diplomatic and economic ties with other nations, positioning itself as a key player in addressing global challenges and promoting international cooperation.

Conclusion

Throughout our journey, we've explored Mexico's rich history, diverse culture, and stunning landscapes. We've seen the ancient wonders, enjoyed the vibrant festivals, and tasted the delicious cuisine that makes Mexico unique.

Mexico's future is bright with its focus on sustainable development, educational reforms, and technological growth. This country isn't just preserving its heritage but also looking ahead to a promising future.

As young readers, continue to discover more about this incredible country. Let the stories of Mexico inspire you to explore, learn, and appreciate the world around you. Viva México!

Made in the USA
Las Vegas, NV
30 November 2024

13018189R00069